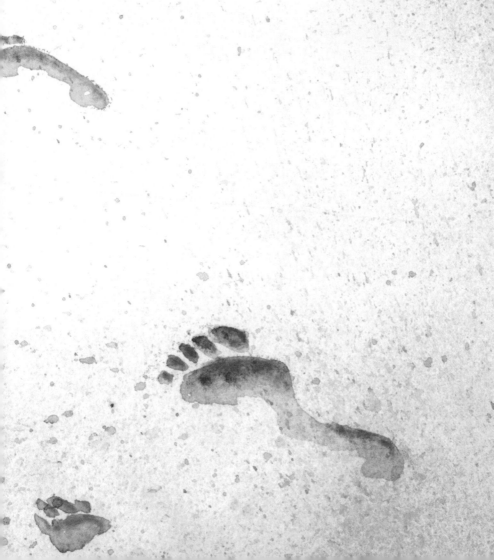

i'm still here

To my beloved husband, W. Bruce Cameron,

Who so wanted me to open my heart to another dog that he told me the story that became *A Dog's Purpose*, which has helped millions open their hearts to another dog.

And to my beloved dog, Tucker,

Who is the dog we adopted, and who graciously became the model for the gorgeous paintings in this book. You are an angel dog on Earth, and you will be my angel dog forever.

i'm still here

a dog's purpose
forever

cathryn michon

illustrations by seth taylor

Andrews McMeel
PUBLISHING®

i'm still *here*

the most important thing
you need to understand
you need to feel
to hear
to see
to taste
to smell

(i think smell is always
the best way to know)

is that i'm still *here*
i'm still your dog

it seems like i left
and in a way i did
my fur, my paws, my tail, my breath

they left

but i'm still *here*

right by your side

i walk with you

i sleep with you
i dream with you

(dreams are the best
because we run and run
and you never get tired
of throwing the *ball*
and i never get tired
of chasing it)

if you really listen
you'll hear the scratch of my claws

on the floor

sometimes you do hear it

i can tell

you'll turn your head
and i can tell you're wondering

is that me?

it's me!

the good part is

wherever you go
i go with you

every
single
time

we're not apart
i just don't have my dog body
i do have my dog soul

(which is truly my best part)

always with you
always loving you

i know you feel it when you're dreaming
i just want to convince you
to feel it when you're

awake

because

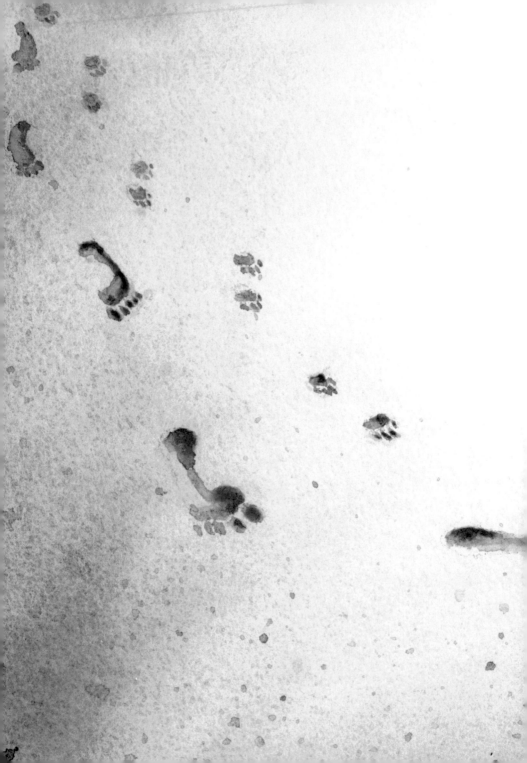

i

am

still

here

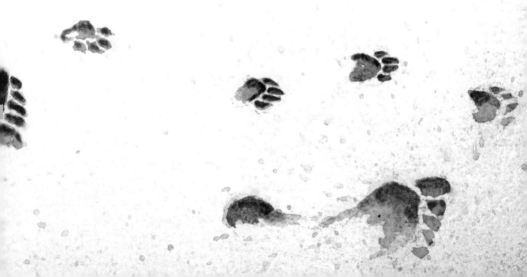

it may seem strange that
i'm
still *here*
because i'm also

                                        there

                              there is wonderful
                                 we feel no pain
                              when we are *there*
                                  all the people
                                 all the animals
                                 you loved *here*
                                  are *there!*

don't worry about that

we're all waiting for you

watching you
loving you
guiding you

when people

cross over

the bridge

your dog and your people
come *here* and *fetch* you!

when you arrive *there*
all the souls you love come running

the people shout words like

welcome!
we missed you!
mom!
dad!
heaven!

and everyone runs and runs
and plays and plays
and sleeps and sleeps
we're never hungry
but there are always

treats!

just like *here*
dogs can smell all the feelings
of the people

                                        there

the feelings are

glee, bliss, peace

it's the way people *here* feel
when they say words like

                  happy birthday!
                trick or treat!
                    dinner!

but *there*

those are the feelings all the time

(actually, dogs
feel like that
most of the time
whether
they're *here* or *there*)

which is what makes *there* so incredible
because dogs spend a lot of their time

here

trying to get people to see
that they should feel the way dogs do

happy to be *here*
or *there*

when we're *there*

                                      after a while

dogs come back

                  here

                  i assume people come back
                    people are so amazing
                      how could they not?
            people can do so many things
                they can take their own

                        car rides!

        that's how amazing people are

but dogs
are no more in charge
of when we come back
than we are of *car rides*

which is why

i'm
still
here

words are not *barks*
dogs *bark*
that is like, so known
but our *barks* are just that

barks

they're not words
words are what people do

all of a sudden

(sometimes without a thought)

a *bark* (or many *barks*)
just wants to come out of me
and when it does
it's glorious
it can be hard to stop
but really

why stop?

the only reason to stop
is to make a person happy
but sometimes
the need to *bark*
this deep, aching well of need to *bark*
cannot be stopped

the *bark* must happen

words
on the other hand
turn out to mean things

like for example

chicken

means

chicken!

it can be very helpful
in the love between people and dogs
when we figure out your words

instantly
we know what you want
or what you have

as in the case of *chicken*

there are so many words i adore

chicken

(i know i mentioned it,
but it's worth repeating)

go for a walk
is a great word
good dog
is probably the best word

bath
no
leave it

those are not my favorites

but in my experience
life is always more about
good dog
than
bath

dogs don't need words
because we can smell feelings
like happy, or sad

we can also smell *chicken*

(i don't want to make it
seem like *chicken*
is the most important word
but i don't want to
mislead you either)

       chicken
is an extremely important word!

actually, though,
the feeling words
are the most important

words like

love you
good dog

if there were suddenly less words

                        i would pick

            good dog

                as being the best one

sit

is not my favorite word

not at all

sit

isn't a thing
or a feeling
it's a trick dogs do
and it's excruciatingly hard

sit

means
don't be a dog
for a while
and it can be a long while

sit

means
though my hind legs are vibrating
with the need to run
to feel my claws
dig so satisfyingly into dirt, or carpet,
or just anything
and propel my mighty legs forward
with the pure ecstasy of movement

instead, i must tell my legs
(which were made for running)
not to run
which seems absurd

but

sit

makes any person happy
(which is all i have ever wanted)

sit

means i'm a *good dog*

so i do it

i *sit*

until i'm such a *good dog*
that i don't have to do

sit

anymore

if you think *sit* is bad
wait until you hear

stay

once a dog figures out what

stay

means
we start to think

people can't be serious
about this

they can't possibly take
something as ridiculous as

sit

and somehow make it worse

well, they can

because that's

stay

people often repeat it

stay

stay

stay

i guess because *stay* is so dreadful
that dogs really can't believe it

stay

i mean really

but *good dogs* like me

will do it
we are that good

that's how good we are
the dogs who *stay*

i do know
dogs don't live as long as people
it could be because people
don't do joy
as much as dogs

joy wears dogs out
but in a good way

sometimes i have so much

joy

that i get
what people call *zoomies*
after that
i need a nap
but since i love naps
it all works out

maybe another reason
dogs don't live as long
is so we can show you
how to

cross over
from *here* to *there*

so you can see
it's no big deal

we go first
so we can guide you

dogs are good at that
you always act
like you're walking us

good one!

we're actually walking you

one thing about life *here*
i will never understand
is what people call

the cone of shame

i'll just be living my best dog life
minding my own business
sniffing all the sniffs
and suddenly a person puts me in

the cone of shame

then, when i'm out for a walk
people see me, and they say

the cone of shame! the cone of shame!

like i'm some kind of *bad dog*
but i'm not!

and the worst thing about it is
i'll have an

itch

i absolutely need to scratch
but *the cone of shame*
literally makes it impossible
which is another bad thing about

the cone of shame

obviously, people have no idea
about that part
or they would never put it on us

eventually the time of
the cone of shame
comes to an end

not one moment too soon

being a puppy
never gets old
run, run, run
chew, chew, chew
nap

learn tricks
that make no sense like

do your business

(people get very worked up
about that one)
eventually you realize it means don't lift your leg
or squat inside

it's beyond confusing

leash

is just nuts
and involves people saying

                                                        bad dog

a lot
which upsets everyone

as a puppy

to pull on my *leash*
is so logical
and feels fantastic
but people do not like it
so eventually i stop pulling

now that i'm *here*

watching you
(without my dog body)

i'm pulling you
toward appreciating

more

worrying

less

i'm pulling you

(like a *bad dog* puppy
who can't do *leash*)

toward happiness

just with my thoughts

can you feel it?

i used to think that very small people
were like puppies
but they're not
for one thing, they cry more
(like, a lot more)

but

very small people

are
the easiest people
to adore
because
a dog's purpose
is reminding people
to have more fun

and

very small people

are so there for that

do you remember

when we first met?
i know i do
i drank in the intoxicating scent of you
that i now know so well
it's the

you smell

you're the only one in the world
who has it

when you are coming, the

you smell

can wake me
from the deepest sleep
i love it even better than *treats*
you are the *treat*
i crave most

i remember
when we first met
i gleefully trembled
at that first touch
of your hand on my fur
it let me know

i was *home*

we belonged to each other
we both knew it
we'll always know it

when we meet again
it will be just the same
i'll drink it in again

the

you smell

it's everything
because you are everything

if i could give dogs advice
i would tell them
one thing i've learned is

don't
chew
shoes

seriously, just don't

it makes people crazy

though shoes are delicious

we should talk
about when you pet me

how do you know?

oh, you know
exactly where to place
your splendid fingers
which are saturated
with the tantalizing smells
of *cheese* and flowers

to scratch my butt

or stroke the exact right spot
behind my ears
where i struggle to reach

oh yes!

it's right there, yes!

then i roll on my back
and your perfect palms
gently *belly rub* me
(exactly where
i'm longing to be rubbed)
how do you know?

you know because

you
are
magic

there are a few things i miss
about being in a dog body
crinkly wrappers
is one

it starts
with the large cold door
that opens with a whoosh
of delectable scents
i don't know all the words of the scents
but words like
chicken
cheese
bacon
come to mind

you reach in
pull out a block
you kneel down to me
then you crinkle the crinkly wrapper
finally revealing that luscious *cheese*

       cheese is another word
       i can't get enough of

unlike

          bath

(which as i've said
i could totally do without)

you use your miraculous hands
to remove the crinkly wrapper

(you know,
i could do a lot
with hands like yours
instead of paws,
just saying)

as you hold out the *cheese*

my tongue
            (which has only ever
            brought me good news)
begins
                    licking my lips

i can't help it

you say the word *gentle*
and i know what that means

so carefully, tenderly
i take the *cheese*
with the very edge of my lips
the softest nibble of my teeth
the scent fills my nose
the taste explodes

                              on my tongue

i wiggle in sheer delight

because that tiny piece of *cheese*
tastes exactly like love

your love
for me

there's a fun trick
all dogs *there* can do it
(people *there* can do it too)
we reach out with our thoughts to

things with wings

(who are *here*)

and we ask them to say hello to you

and they do it!
they are very persistent, these
things with wings

hello! hello!

that's what they are saying

they will not leave you alone
until you notice them

so, when

things with wings

won't leave you alone

you should know

that is someone *there*

saying

hello to you!

please say hello back

we all love it!

only a creature
as marvelous as a person
could come up with an object
as magnificent as a *ball*

squeeze it in your teeth
and you'll see what i mean

the best part
is that you want that *ball*
as much as i do
you throw the *ball*
(momentarily pretending
you don't want it)

good one!

then i fly through the air
and catch it
with a satisfying squish in my jaws

i race to bring it back
and we're both
so
delighted
by the pretense
of you not wanting it
that we do it again and again
until it leads to a nap

when we do *ball*
together
we just focus on

ball

ball is now

ball is all
that matters

ball, ball, ball

if you ever doubt
people are the best
just think of

ball

sometimes i wonder
if people can't smell
as well as dogs

which would be so sad
because obviously sniffs and smells are the best
part of life
when you're *here*

(i mean, how else would you know
what people and dogs are feeling?)

it's so important
to be able to smell

anger
and love
and fear

here's something good to know:

the smells *there* are even better

here
the smell of *fried chicken*
instantly causes me to drool
licking my lips
in eager anticipation
of the splendor of
fried chicken

but *there* it smells even better!

also, *there*

i'm always allowed to have
as much as i want

but people *here*
or even *there*
don't seem to sniff each other
like it matters at all
(which it obviously does)
i feel sorry for people; they do their best

you may have noticed
my tail has a mind of its own

wait

that's not it
my tail is actually connected
straight to my soul
and our souls live forever

thump, thump, thump

can you hear it?
that's my tail saying
exactly what my soul
feels for you
right now

it's my opinion
that people are too afraid
too much of the time
dogs fear terrible things like *baths*
but once we're doing *bath*
we don't stay afraid
we get over it

it always works out fine in the end
people smell scared when nothing scary is even
happening

no *bath* in sight

fear is not good for you
so dogs try to help people
get over it

fear chases away love
fear chases away joy
fear chases away life

my advice to people:
live life like the dogs
fear less, love more

if i were as sublime of a creature

as a person

i would have more *toys*

everywhere i looked
   there would be things to chew
   and shake!

   not *bad dog* things like shoes

   (which are not *toys*
   as i have explained)

i would have so many *toys*
that are *good dog* to tear apart

(because every dog knows
that tearing apart
is what *toys* are best for)

it's very surprising

that creatures as powerful

as people

don't seem to have anything

to tear apart

people almost have no *toys* at all

maybe it's proof of how much

they love dogs

that they give us

all the *toys*

people are so wondrous
they open doors
they know where to find the food
dogs are so impressed

with people

you love us so perfectly
that's why we'll be waiting for you

on the happy day you
cross over
the bridge

but you should know

how much we appreciate
when you help us

cross over

since we usually go first

we do our best
to let you know
it's time to help us

cross over

please understand
that when you help dogs

cross over

the one thing we know for sure is

you gave us the best life ever

we only remember
the *ear scratches*
the *belly rubs*
the *car rides*
the *treats*

we never even think about
the *baths*

you loved us perfectly
in every way

thank you

there are things i do sometimes
that people don't even know i'm doing

for example
most people need a mate
but sometimes
(i'm sorry to say)
they're pretty bad
at finding a good one

it's almost like
they aren't using their noses
to sniff out what is
undeniable

a bad mate smells as bad
as a dog who's just had a *bath*

oh, it's bad, all right

dogs know

i do my best
to help people understand
what they should be able to smell for themselves

stay away from that one

sometimes it works
(always listen to the dog
our nose knows)

there's something i need you to know

or maybe to remember

you are always loved
by me
by other people
by other creatures

by whoever is in charge
of *here* and *there*

the reason i mention it is
               i think sometimes you forget
but if you remember nothing else
               remember this:

               you are so loved

it was maybe my greatest purpose
when i was *here* in my dog body
to remind you of this

it's still my greatest purpose
i'm still reminding you

you are so loved

i have lived in dog bodies
many times
sometimes i was big
which was great for catching *balls*

sometimes i was small
which made me the boss

of course

i remember all my lives

and my people

the best
is when i come back to you
in a different dog body

when i

crossed over

from *here* to *there*
my very last thought was

i want you to get another dog

it might be me!

(or they might send my friend)

no matter what

it will be a *good dog*

all dog souls are different
but they are all *good dogs*

when a dog is sad, or mad, or even bad
it doesn't last
it's just not how we're made
because
we're not as complicated as people

it doesn't take long
for us to remember
that we love all people
it only takes one good person
to make us remember that

of course

it's
a dog's purpose
to love people

that's how we're made

and we're loving people best
when we can guide you to happy

we can sniff happy out
like it's *bacon*
and lead you right to it

as long as you pay attention

a trick i really loved doing
when i was *here*,
in a dog body,
was

take your own leash and go home

i would take my *leash* in my mouth
and then run to a door

                        and then i'd get a *treat!*
it wasn't always the same door

                        but it was fun to run
                    and fun to shake my *leash*
               and fun to be in charge of my *leash*

(which isn't how *leashes* work
most of the time)

crossing over

from *here* to *there*
reminds me of that trick
i loved so much

take your own leash and go home

the trick is fun because you run with joy
toward something wonderful

home

home is a word that makes people smell happy
maybe *home* is just another word
for any happy place
like

there

which is the happiest place
i've ever been

i just want you to know
that when you are

crossing over

from *here* to *there*
it will be as much fun as the trick

take your own leash and go home

and i will be your *treat*

everyone you loved will be your *treat*
when you are *there* with us

there is *home*

and we will be waiting

don't worry
don't be fooled
our souls never stop
your soul is precious to me
you are this dog's purpose

forever

and that is why

i'm

still

here

Afterword

I never met Cathryn Michon's first and only dog, Ellie, though I did name a character after that Doberman in *A Dog's Purpose*. It was only fitting: if it hadn't been for Ellie, I never would have written that novel in the first place.

I had moved out to Los Angeles for work and was starting to "see" this beautiful woman, Cathryn. By "see" I mean "date," though I was arguably too old for such nonsense, and I *knew* I was too old to meet her parents when she suggested we take that step.

So, we were driving from LA to San Francisco to "meet the parents." I hoped her dad would be nicer than Robert De Niro. Cathryn turned to me in the middle of the drive and shockingly stated, "I will never have another dog. I can't go through losing a dog again."

I knew from sad experience of the pain and grief that comes from losing a canine companion, but I also knew the joy of adopting a new dog—a heart's refill. How could I convince her that a dog's love is worth it, and that the same love she had from Ellie was available to her from another dog if only she tried again?

Because I communicate through storytelling, I made up a tale on the spot about a dog who never dies, but reincarnates, learning lessons through each life that enable him to return and save his original boy.

A dog's love, you see, is always unconditional, always wonderful, and maybe, if you're particularly observant, you might realize that your new dog is your old best friend, returned to you after death.

Well, she did understand, and we did get another dog, Tucker, who was the model for the angel dog in this beautiful book. I always say she liked the story so much, she married me.

Both Tucker and I are grateful.

—W. Bruce Cameron

Acknowledgments

I must thank my super-agent, Jane Dystel, for cheering for this project from day one, and for getting me to the remarkable Jean Lucas, who expertly guided it every step of the way. What an honor it is to be published by Andrews McMeel, and I want to thank the entire team there who have been perfect in every possible way. My illustrator, Seth Taylor, is very talented and, more importantly, loves dogs, and I'm grateful for all his work. Also thanks to Dode Levenson for graphic magic. I must thank my brilliant husband, W. Bruce Cameron, for telling me (and then the world) about a dog soul who reincarnates, slipping from Earth to heaven and back, but who eternally remembers and loves his people. Finally, thanks to my dog, Tucker, for not only being the best dog in the whole world (except for all the other dogs) but also for being the model for many of these paintings as well as being our cover boy. He liked doing all of it except for the stuff in the bath. Sorry about that one, buddy . . .

—Cathryn Michon

Thank you to my Mom, Dad, Frank, and Fritz for showing me a creative life was possible, giving me the tools, and trusting me to find my way.

Thanks to my agent, John Rudolph, even keeled in every storm.

Thanks to Molly, GR, Boecephus, Mr. Z, Leon, GD, Esme, Penny, Kumgangi, and Eumguangi for guiding my heart. Thanks to Custer who stayed just long enough.

And to Byeong Yeon and Mina who fill my heart with light.

—Seth Taylor

Andrews McMeel Publishing
a division of Andrews McMeel Universal
1130 Walnut Street, Kansas City, Missouri 64106

www.andrewsmcmeel.com

24 25 26 27 28 TEN 10 9 8 7 6 5 4 3 2

ISBN: 978-1-5248-9381-1

Library of Congress Control Number: 2024931859

Editor: Jean Z. Lucas
Art Director: Holly Swayne
Production Editor: Brianna Westervelt
Production Manager: Chadd Keim

ATTENTION: SCHOOLS AND BUSINESSES
Andrews McMeel books are available at quantity discounts
with bulk purchase for educational, business, or sales promotional use.
For information, please e-mail the Andrews McMeel Publishing
Special Sales Department: sales@amuniversal.com.